So you'd think we'd all be determined to get mighty good at picking and choosing people. If this is *the* cornerstone for success as a leader, then why shouldn't we find the very best methodology and work relentlessly to master it?

Well, we should. And the approach you're looking for is laid out in this handbook. It's based on the master work in the field—the *Topgrading* hardback that's sold over 100,000 copies—together with the 40+ years of combined experience Brad and Geoff Smart bring to the table.

Brad's been a dear friend since the beginning of my professional career when we worked at the same firm. I've known Geoff since the day he was born. The extreme talent, high drive, and finely tuned expertise of these two professionals epitomize what it means to be an *A player*. They're the best in the business. Unquestionably.

They'll both tell you, "Recruiting and selecting the kind of talent that can assure your success has never been a cakewalk, and never will be." It takes know-how. Practice. Discipline. *Topgrading* gives you the technique. It's the proven, premier methodology for producing high talent teams. Now the rest is up to you.

Just keep this in mind: *Topgrading is a career-maker.* Pick the right people, and your success is practically guaranteed.

— *Price Pritchett, Ph.D.*

PRITCHETT

With more than 10,000 talent assessments under their belts, Brad and Geoff Smart are authorities on selecting top performers. Their work with a broad range of organizations—including GE, Honeywell, Lincoln Financial Group, and the American Heart Association—has helped them develop Topgrading as the platinum standard for talent assessment.

Chapter 1

What is
TOPGRADING?

TOPGRADING simply means filling every position in your organization with an *A player.*

Now that sounds like a pretty straightforward concept. But right here we see the first two aspects of the Topgrading approach that make it starkly different from common hiring practices.

First, you target only the *best people.* Top tier candidates. Ideally, nobody else is even allowed in the running. At the very outset you try to limit the field of possible contenders to *A players.* Just think about that. Rather than follow the conventional practice of more or less open field competition, you narrow it down from the beginning. You restrict the pool of potential candidates to high talent. Pull this off, and it essentially guarantees that you'll end up with a high performer. After all, the less promising people don't even get admitted to the tryouts.

Second, Topgrading means you follow this practice in filling *every position.* Not just for a couple of key slots. Not just when you randomly get lucky and a bunch of great candidates throw their hats into the ring. You adhere to the same talent standards across the board—wall-to-wall, top-to-bottom. Doesn't matter whether you're trying to fill a slot on the shipping dock, out in the field, for the middle management ranks, or in the executive suite. You maintain the same discipline in your selection process.

"The toughest decisions in organizations are people decisions—hiring, firing, promotion, etc. These are the decisions that receive the least attention and are the hardest to *unmake*."

— Peter Drucker

Chapter 2

Calculate your cost
OF MIS-HIRES.

What do you *really* have at stake when you hire?

You need to consider the question from two angles—the upside payoff in hiring an ace, and the downside potential if the person fails. The difference between the star and the failure is the risk gap. It shows what you have on the line in the personnel selection process, and it'll make you a true believer in Topgrading.

For most positions, what you pay in salary is not the most important number. What you should give the most attention to are (1) how much value a high talent person could reasonably bring, versus (2) how big the cost could be from weak performance and having to replace a failure.

Our calculations consistently show that the average cost of mis-hiring can be *15 times base salary.* We can detail this out for you. We've done it hundreds of times for clients—using *their* numbers—and they're always staggered by the true cost of their "ordinary" hiring practices.

Let's consider, for example, a mid-manager whose salary is in the $100,000 range. At 15 times base salary, a hiring mistake carries a $1.5 million price tag, when both actual and opportunity costs are included. And it's the same story for internal promotions that don't pan out.

Calculate your cost of mis-hires.

Mistakes with incumbents are usually about as expensive as mis-hiring an external candidate.

When you realize how much money is riding on your employment decisions, you rapidly lose patience with conventional approaches.

Imagine, that in order to get these costs under control, your company decides to take a Six Sigma approach to assessing talent. What this means is that you'll strive for no more than 4.5 defects per million in your hiring and promoting practices. But most companies say they're less than 25 percent successful at hiring externally or promoting internally. In Six Sigma terminology, this translates to an alarming rate of 750,000 defects per million! What would the impact be if your company tolerated this defect rate in products or customers?

Also, think about the collateral damage caused by the puny 25 percent success rate in replacing underperformers. The disruption is huge. For example, replacing 40 people to achieve 90 percent *A players* would require hiring 141 replacements—and firing or redeploying 101 of them. No board of directors would permit such a revolving door. And, by the way, what *A player* would want to join this massacre-prone company?

If your organization uses typical assessment methods that select only 25 percent *A's* or *A potentials* when replacing lesser talent, you can NEVER achieve more than two-thirds *A players*. So the answer has to be: IMPROVE YOUR SUCCESS RATE!

Topgrading Calculator

Total Number of Replacements to Achieve 90 Percent *A Players*

Number of Underperformers To Be Replaced	Your Current Success in Hiring/Promoting			
	25%	50%	75%	90%
10	31	17	11	10
20	67	35	24	20
40	141	72	48	40
100	357	179	120	100

Look at it strictly from a financial angle, and you'll see that it makes no sense to settle for low quality hiring. You don't save money when you use second or third rate selection processes. And you don't get a bargain when you give your jobs to the weaker candidates who'll come for a little less money.

Those kinds of compromises cost you dreadfully more in the long run.

"The easiest job in the world has to be coroner. Surgery on dead people. What's the worst thing that could happen? If everything went wrong, maybe you'd get a pulse."

— Dennis Miller

"A's hire A's, B's hire C's."

— Donald Rumsfeld,
former CEO of GD Searle & Company,
and twice U. S. Secretary of Defense

Chapter 3

Begin Topgrading from
THE TOP DOWN.

TOPGRADING works at any level of the organization, but it always needs to be implemented top-down. Why is this so important? *A players* hire *A players. B* and *C players* hire *B's* and *C's.*

There are several reasons why it always seems to play out this way. First, the *Non-A* managers just may not recognize talent when they see it. That's the sort of thing that keeps them from being *A's.* Of course, sometimes they just flat don't *care* enough. They set lower standards in general, and this manifests itself in how they hire. All too often, though, it comes down to the fact that they don't feel safe hiring someone that might threaten them. Basically, *B* and *C players* fear Topgrading. It makes them nervous to be in a crowd of *A*-types, because at least they're savvy enough to know they could easily look weak in comparison. Their solution is to find safety in a mob of mediocrity.

Strategically, you need a critical mass of *A players* at the top to drive and sustain your Topgrading effort. So start by building this coalition. Launch your Topgrading initiative with a solid team of *A players* at the top, and the rest of the organization will get the message that you're serious about building a Topgrading culture. They'll also hear, loud and clear, that Topgrading is not the flavor of the month, but a business process that's here to stay.

If you're Topgrading your entire company, start with the executive team. In this case, the CEO should be the Topgrading champion. That's the person who needs to articulate the business reasons for implementing Topgrading. It's also critical that the CEO model and enforce Topgrading practices with his or her direct reports.

The same principle applies if you're implementing Topgrading within your division or department. Once again, start with your top team. In this case, you become the "Division CEO." You must assume most of the responsibilities listed for the CEO above. However, rather than publicly broadcasting your intention to Topgrade, it's probably better to take a "stealth approach." Quietly begin the process of redeploying *B* and *C players* and replacing them with *A's*. This approach will avoid triggering the cultural antibodies in your organization and help minimize resistance.

Once you've Topgraded your top team, there are four other best practices you'll need to learn and implement.

> First, conduct a *Talent Review* of everyone on your team.
> Second, create *Scorecards* for each key role.
> Third, build your *Virtual Bench* of *A players* and *A potentials* to meet your future hiring needs.
> Finally, learn how to conduct three different types of interviews: *Screening interviews, Topgrading interviews,* and *Reference Check interviews.*

These best practices should improve your hiring and promoting success rate from 25 percent to 90 percent. Maybe better.

Initially, implementing Topgrading takes time and energy. But unlike the busywork of micromanaging *B* and *C players,* Topgrading pays huge dividends down the line.

"If you lose your job, your marriage and your mind all in the same week, try to lose your mind first, because then the other stuff won't matter that much."

— **Jack Handey**

"Those who build great companies under-
stand that the ultimate throttle on growth
for any great company is not markets,
or technology, or competition, or products.
It is the one thing above all others; the
ability to get and keep enough of the
right people."

— Jim Collins, *Good to Great*

Chapter 4

Conduct a Talent Review to identify your
A PLAYERS.

The purpose of a Talent Review is to distinguish your *A's* and *A potentials* from your *Non-A's*. *A potentials* have the right stuff, but need to be developed. *Non-A's* are the *B's* and *C's*.

The first step in the review process is to rank order all your employees from Most Valuable Player to Least Valuable Player. Then you assign ratings, designating each person as an *A player, A potential,* or *Non-A.* Rating and ranking all your employees on a regular basis helps you sustain a Topgrading mentality. It's also quite revealing.

The evaluation will position you to develop action items regarding what to do next with each employee. It provides a general roadmap for your coaching, development, and redeployment activities. For example, identifying your *A players* highlights who you need to support. Labeling your *A potentials* shows who you need to coach. Acknowledging your *Non-A's* reveals who you need to move into a different role or move out of the organization.

This represents solid, hard-core management on your part. A realistic and unvarnished Talent Review keeps you honest about the Topgrading process. Without it, the program can begin to lose discipline and start to drift. You need this regular scrutiny just to track how people are progressing and to calibrate your talent management efforts.

As you go through this drill, you'll also want to identify any open positions, soon-to-be-open positions, or new positions that need to be filled. This prepares you to launch timely, effective searches. It also focuses you on the available slots that might offer the right kind of promotion or transfer opportunities for your incumbents.

Don't worry about getting the ratings perfect on your first Talent Review. Just be honest and fair. Most managers are afraid their first Talent Review will expose a team profile that's 25 percent *A's,* 50 percent *B's,* and 25 percent *C's.* In fact, Topgrading professionals would more likely rate the same team as having at least 50 percent *A's* and *A potentials.* That's because they're more experienced at seeing the hidden talent of square-peg people who've been put in round-hole jobs. They also have more experience in determining when a person could be relieved of some responsibilities, perhaps accompanied by a reduction in pay, to become an *A player* again.

Be sure to set goals for improving your percentage of *A players* and *A potentials.* But don't make the common mistake of thinking all *A's* have to be *promotable.* Some of your *A's* will have the potential to assume bigger and more complex responsibilities. Others may remain solid *role players* for the majority of their career. Both are *A players.* Both are creating value in their jobs and making life easier for you.

How many promotable *A's* you need depends on how fast your company is growing. If you're growing at double-digit rates, you'll need a healthy stable of promotable *A's.* If your growth is less aggressive, you may need more solid role players. Just remember *A's* are *A's* and treat them as such.

Topgrading

"When you go for a job interview,
   I think a good thing to ask is if they
   ever press charges."
                            — Jack Handey

"Studies suggest that with knowledge workers, the difference in productivity between a top performer and an average or below average performer is over 100%, whereas in assembly line workers it's 20%. Since there are more knowledge workers today, better talent in these positions creates much more value."

— **Ed Michaels, Former Director of McKinsey & Company**
From *The War for Talent Study*

Chapter 5

Create Scorecards that guarantee accountability AND FIT.

SCORECARD is not just a fancy name for a job description. It's a different creature in two important ways. First, a well crafted Scorecard quantifies the *key accountabilities* that define *A*-level performance in a specific job. Second, a Scorecard clarifies the *competencies* that define a "good fit" between the candidate and that position.

These are important criteria for two people in particular—you, and the person you eventually hire. If you design it with precision and detail, the Scorecard will powerfully guide the recruiting process, shape your hiring decision, then focus both you and the candidate on the most critical performance issues from day one.

Of course, managers ordinarily rely on conventional job descriptions to serve these purposes. But what's missing in standard practice is the "grading" component. Job descriptions have no teeth!

Check it out. Most job descriptions are little more than a list of tasks the jobholder must perform, plus a guess at what profile a successful candidate might have.

Create Scorecards that guarantee accountability and fit.

For a Key Account Sales Manager, a traditional job description might say:

- Must be effective at capturing new accounts
- Must excel at closing business
- Must have excellent communication skills
- Must have three years of relevant sales experience
- Must have a college degree
- Must blah, blah, blah

Notice how that phraseology fails to provide a way to measure the performance you're wanting. How many new accounts must be captured? How much business must be closed? How good do the communication skills have to be? What constitutes relevant experience? Does it matter whether candidates graduated at the top or bottom of their college class? Scorecards make explicit what job descriptions leave to interpretation.

Scorecards define specifically, with metrics attached, what *A*-level performance looks like in a particular job. They let job candidates know, in no uncertain terms, what they'll be responsible for delivering. Scorecards don't merely talk. They can bite.

And guess what...*A players* love this kind of accountability! *B* and *C* players, on the other hand, head for the hills. "You want me to take ownership...YIKES! You can actually measure whether I'm succeeding or failing...NOWHERE TO HIDE! You want me to stretch...THINK I'LL PASS."

So, not only do Scorecards help you attract *A players*, they simultaneously repel *Non-A players*. Perfect. The system is working. If you're serious about building a performance culture, start by creating Scorecards that guarantee accountability and fit.

"I always arrive late at the office,
but I make up for it by leaving early."

— Charles Lamb

"Leaders of great groups love talent and know where to find it. They revel in the talent of others."

— Warren Bennis & Patricia Ward
in *Organizing Genius*

Chapter 6

Strengthen your
VIRTUAL BENCH.

Your Topgrading ambitions won't survive without a continuous flow of talent coming your way.

This isn't a one-time thing. You can staff up to a straight-*A* team, but sooner or later somebody's going to leave. Or get promoted. Maybe the job even outgrows the incumbent. For one reason or another, you'll be looking for a new person. A key part of being a Topgrader is having good people waiting in the wings.

To be successful at this you need to become a relentless talent scout. Recruitment has to take its place as part of your everyday consciousness. Tune your attention to hunt for winners, to be on the lookout for *A players* all the time. High talent can show up almost anywhere in the social landscape. On an airplane, at a wedding, in some conference crowd or business meeting, maybe at a friend's party, or at your kid's sporting event. Do this right, and you won't even be reading newspapers and trade journals the same as before. You'll be spotting people who are winning awards, getting promotions, or being assigned heavy duty projects. If you're sensitized to finding *A players,* you'll start to see them everywhere.

Then go out of your way to get to know these people. Develop a personal relationship with each one. And how many *A* candidates should you shoot for in this group? Depends on several different things—the size of your operation, its growth rate, your turnover statistics, and so on. But your bench should be big enough to hold a lot more talent than you expect to need in the foreseeable future.

The point we're emphasizing is that chasing down good people should be something you *personally* commit to doing. What about recruiters and search firms? They're okay in a pinch. But you may spend as much time and energy managing them as you would identifying candidates on your own. It also will cost you a whole lot more with no guarantee of any better results. CEOs say when they pay for a search, they're disappointed with the results 79 percent of the time.

Presumably you can go to your HR department. It's their job to find you good candidates, right? Sure, they should be able to help. But if you miss your objectives, don't expect your boss to accept the excuse that "HR didn't find me enough qualified candidates."

How about internal candidates? Don't good companies promote from within? You bet. Managers should use tandem interviews and discussions with co-workers to screen internal candidates. But what if *A's* or *A potentials* don't pass this test? Or what if someone does, but internal politics eliminates the person?

We're not saying you shouldn't use search firms, or rely on HR to help you recruit, or try to promote from within. We're simply insisting that you'll need to augment those sources with your strong Virtual Bench. You'll also benefit from requiring your direct reports to develop their Virtual Bench as well.

Having this kind of talent pipeline is a strategic asset for your career. Just don't wait until you have an urgent need to begin building your bench. Start today by asking every *A player* you know to introduce you to an *A player* they know. These could be *A's* you might hire in the future, or people who can recommend other candidates to you. It's primarily through your *A player* network that you'll find the top performers you need.

As the feeder system for your Topgrading future, this Virtual Bench requires constant attention. Relationships can grow cold. You can lose contact as people move about. So make sure you schedule one meaningful touch point per week with at least one of your Virtual Bench members. That touch point can be lunch, a phone call, a meeting at the airport—whatever makes sense to you. Yes, it's work. But it's part of your job, and it's an investment that'll make things go easier and more successfully for you in the future.

"Oh, you hate your job? Why didn't you say so? There's a support group for that. It's called EVERYBODY, and they meet at the bar." — Drew Carey

"If a guy has a really good success pattern, I'll go along with him if he says he can go to the moon on Scotch tape."

— Raymond Herzog, former CEO, 3M Company

Chapter 7

Interview to
identify performance
PATTERNS.

Interviewing typically plays a key role in the candidate evaluation process. Everybody does it. But most organizations' interview practices are crippled by a fundamental weakness: *They're not predictive of job performance.*

Big problem. And it explains why even sophisticated global 100 companies, using a series of one-hour competency interviews, have an 80 percent failure rate.

If your interview data is so incomplete or inconclusive that it fails to provide a sound basis for prediction, you're just shooting in the dark. Vague information leads to shallow analysis. And that combination has a strong chance of causing another costly mis-hire.

Now, interviews remain the centerpiece in the Topgrading process. But *this* approach has tremendous muscle. No more rambling conversations with candidates. No more confusion about your interviewing agenda. And none of this lightweight questioning that shies away from sensitive issues which often count the most. Topgrading interviews are carefully sequenced, tightly structured, and aimed squarely at topics with the richest information payload. No soft spots, no wasted motion.

Interview to identify performance patterns.

Topgrading brings true professionalism to your interviewing. You collect enough data, in the right order, with the rigor and discipline necessary for predictive patterns of performance to emerge. The line of inquiry has an elegant efficiency marked by simplicity and unusual depth. It brings to the surface the most meaningful aspects of a person's background. You start to see trends. You capture hard evidence of the candidate's achievements and capabilities. Piercing insights come to you about the individual's current makeup and future potential. As the data systematically accumulates, you can see how past is prologue. You know what's coming if this person gets hired. You can *predict*.

These predictive patterns are the "active ingredient" that makes the Topgrading methodology so potent. And they don't happen by accident. You could shoot the bull with a candidate for several hours and never pick up the scent of crucial strengths or weaknesses. Even if you consider yourself a tough interviewer, you can miss critical elements that the Topgrading approach would easily bring into the picture. The most precious information is that which sharpens your predictive power. And that's the data you produce when you follow the Topgrading roadmap.

It takes practice. But you'll learn to recognize and interpret these predictive patterns of performance. Most people need to conduct at least a dozen or more interviews to become proficient in these techniques. As the mechanics of the interviewing become second nature, you'll be able to focus your attention more on looking for the critical patterns that the Topgrading process exposes so effectively. It's this more sophisticated level of observation, interpretation, and analysis of performance patterns that distinguishes Topgrading from traditional interviewing techniques.

There are three types of interviews you'll need to master:

- Screening
- Topgrading
- Reference Check

Screening interviews are supposed to feed *A* candidates into the pipeline, plus eliminate *B's* and *C's* early in the process. This gives you more time to compare and contrast *A* candidates so you hire the very best person for the job. Topgrading interviews delve much deeper. They're designed to provide a penetrating look into *A* candidates' capabilities so you can tell which *A* is the most qualified and best fit for the job. Reference Check interviews are designed to confirm your decision to make an offer to a specific *A* candidate. They give you one last checkpoint to validate the candidate's strengths, weaknesses, and potential by talking with people the individual has worked with previously.

Together, the three types of interviews provide an efficient yet thorough process for identifying your most viable candidates.

"This one job said they wanted a college degree or equivalent. I said, 'Perfect, I have eight years of high school.'"

— Buzz Nutley

"There is something rare, something finer far, something much more scarce than ability. It's the ability to recognize ability."

— Elbert Hubbard

Chapter 8

Screen *A's* in, screen out THE *B's* AND *C's*.

Your first pass at sizing up people should be discerning enough to filter out *Non-A* candidates. Topgrading, done right, takes *B's* and *C's* out of the game at the very beginning.

This suggests that your initial screening will accomplish more than most organizations' main interview.

In the Topgrading methodology, "screening" does not imply a superficial, casual, or perfunctory look at a person's qualifications. Instead, it's a serious appraisal. Right off the bat, you're gathering data very purposefully. Questions are designed to penetrate fast and produce answers that are rich with predictive value. The Screening interview isn't the typical breezy, fifteen or twenty minute front end conversation—it'll take about an hour. It's not mainly a social chat to warm up the candidate—it's very job-focused. And you won't be winging it. There's homework to do, and you must come prepared.

To start with, you need a genuine understanding of the position you're looking to fill. The Topgrading tool you count on to give clarity around job requirements is the Scorecard. Unlike the usual job description, a job Scorecard spells out accountabilities. Its metrics specify the results you'll require. The Scorecard defines what *A* performance should look like in the position, and that tells you what to look for in a candidate. It puts you in a position to do informed, legitimate screening.

Screen *A's* in, screen out the *B's* and *C's.*

The second Topgrading tool that plays a big role in your screening process is the Career History Form. You don't want to rely on someone's resume for background data. It's really nothing more than the person's "sales brochure." Likewise, the job application form always leaves way too many questions unanswered.

The Career History Form is a marvelously revealing document. It asks the candidate to account for every year and month since the person began working full-time jobs. That makes it extremely difficult for a person to hide information that you need to know. The form makes specific requests for compensation history, breaking it down into base pay, bonus, and "other" so you don't have to guess. It asks for the name and title of each boss, and makes a clear statement that reference checks will be conducted on finalists (with their permission). This helps inspire honesty.

Dozens of inches of space on the Career History Form are provided for the candidate to record what was liked most and least about prior jobs. The form asks for details about education performance. Considerable space also is allotted for the candidate to itemize personal strengths, then give details about weaker points and areas for improvement.

There's more, but you get the picture. The Career History Form gives you the opportunity to begin identifying patterns of performance during the screening process. It also sets the tone for candidates. They'll see that you're a disciplined, rigorous professional in the way you approach the hiring process. *B* and *C* candidates often realize early on that they won't make the cut, and take themselves out of contention. *A* candidates, on the other hand, recognize that they'll shine under these conditions and appreciate the opportunity to distinguish themselves.

"Topgrading is a proven strategy for hiring

A players and building dream teams.
Companies and individuals who Topgrade
gain a talent advantage—they consistently
outperform the competition and reap the
rewards of excellence."

—Robert H. Bohannon,
Chairman, President, and CEO, Viad Corp

"Topgrading will become a continuous process of
raising the bar in the identification of top and bottom
players to enhance overall organizational vitality."

—Bill Conaty, Senior Vice President, Human Resources,
General Electric

"Brad's pursuit of excellence in
selection and development is
critical in a global business
where individual success is
significantly leveraged in a team
of A players."

—Lewis N. Sears, former Vice President,
Organizational Effectiveness, Citibank

"Topgrading the
American Heart
Association will
help save lives."

—Cass Wheeler, CEO,
American Heart Association

"I've had firsthand experience with Brad and his approach
to finding talent, and fitting the talent to the job's
requirements works. Brad's book demystifies the
concept of Topgrading, and as he draws from
thousands of real experiences, he provides a roadmap
for building successful management teams. I wish
he'd put this on paper a long time ago."

—Joseph C. Lawler, President and CEO, CMGI

What's the most *powerful leadership* skill you can have?

Hands down, it's the ability to produce high talent teams. Nothing else even comes close.

EVERYTHING ABOUT LEADERSHIP —

yes, *everything*—starts with people. You, and the people you gather about you, have to come up with all the rest of what it takes to build and run an organization. Like a strategy...your products or services...the money required to keep the place running...the ideas, energy, and ambition that are needed. Every bit of this is born in the hearts, minds, and day-to-day behavior of human beings. The more talented your people are, the better this "everything else" will be.

And it cuts the other way, too. Surround yourself with weaker people, and you're bound to end up with a weaker everything else.

Good Screening interviews go straight to the point, focusing on four questions. The conversation remains tightly focused on the job—there will be time for bonding with true *A* candidates later.

During the Screening interview you'll explore:

- The candidate's career goals
- What the person is really good at professionally
- What he or she is not so good at, or not interested in doing
- Who the last five bosses were, what each boss would list as the candidate's strengths and weak points, plus the overall rating they'd give the person

Most Screening interviews are conducted by phone. If candidates clear this hurdle, you'll probably want to invite them to visit your company, or at least get together for a face-to-face chat over coffee or lunch. If your screening reveals an *A player* candidate isn't interested in making a career change now, offer to stay in touch and add that person to your *A player* Virtual Bench.

According to consulting firm TalentKeepers, the annual cost of employee turnover in the United States tops *$5 trillion.*

"Mediocrity knows nothing higher than itself, but talent instantly recognizes genius."

— Arthur Conan Doyle

Chapter 9

Use Topgrading interviews to explore candidates' STRENGTHS AND WEAKNESSES.

The next step is to schedule more rigorous Topgrading interviews for candidates who pass your initial screening. Don't cut corners on these second phase interviews. Here's where you need to be at your best, because these sessions will determine your degree of Topgrading success.

The Topgrading interview gives you a fine-grained look at a person's background. Question by question, job by job, you peel away the layers, revealing the underlying patterns of performance. As the interview unfolds over the course of several hours, you gradually piece together a coherent picture that shows what the candidate has done in the past. This is history, but it speaks volumes about the future. You're probing for evidence of *A player* attributes the person will carry into tomorrow.

The interview protocol guides you through the person's background in four important areas: school, work history, career goals, and competencies. This is the most promising territory for insights into *A* candidates' interests, experience, and capabilities. Every question you ask is intended to generate clues about patterns of past perform- ance. Why? Because *past performance is the best predictor of future performance.*

Use Topgrading interviews to explore candidates' strengths and weaknesses.

You're going to ask questions about high school and college (if applicable) to determine high and low points during the formative years. Then you'll ask several questions about each job the person has ever held. These questions are:

- What were you hired to do?
- What were your accomplishments?
- What failures or mistakes were made in this job, and what did you learn from them?
- What talent did you inherit *(A's, A potentials,* and *Non-A's),* what changes did you make to this talent mix, and what talent did you end up with?
- What were the people like that you worked for, and how would they rate you?
- Why did you leave?

Toward the end of the Topgrading interview, you'll want to spend about ten minutes asking about the candidate's career goals. What does the person want and need from the next job, next company, and next boss? And what does he or she want five to ten years from now?

Finally, you'll want to ask some relevant Competency Questions to get more specific information. Chances are the candidate will have answered almost all of your concerns regarding crucial competencies earlier in the interview, so this is simply your opportunity to drill down on any areas where you might still have questions.

The Topgrading interview is not the best time to "sell" the candidate on the job. It's okay to talk briefly about the position and answer any specific questions about it. But save the "selling" for later. Your objective during the Topgrading interview is to gather enough data to figure out

"Topgrading is a *philosophy* and *practice* that clearly distinguishes organizations that desire to reach and maintain world-class status. Brad Smart's selection process is built on technically correct assessment techniques, and validated through years of successful experiences with a wide variety of positions and organizations. It works!

—Mel McCall, Senior Vice President, Human Resources, CompUSA

"Brad narrows the target and then tells you how to hit it. For anyone who believes good people make a difference, this is excellent reading."

—Leslie G. Rudd, CEO, Standard Beverage Corporation

"*The notion of Topgrading is unarguable and compelling. Of course we are entitled to a team made up of all A players— we are already paying for them, and talent wins. Why, then, is the practice of Topgrading so elusive? In this highly readable text, Brad Smart offers a thoughtful and practical exploration of Topgrading—how to identify A players, how to nurture and develop people with the potential to become A's, and how to create a sustaining A culture. Now that Smart has put a name to it, Topgrading will be widely recognized as one of the essential and defining leadership skills.*"

—Stephen Rabinowitz, Chairman, President, and CEO (retired), General Cable Corporation

"Brad helped our differentiation of talent implementation in the '80s and '90s."

—Jack Welch, Chairman and CEO (retired), General Electric

"Topgrading is not just desirable but essential for organizational success in this competitive world. Brad has helped me grow, and has helped DSC evolve from a warehousing company to a growth-oriented, leading edge supply-chain management company."

—Ann Drake, CEO, DSC Logistics

"*Once again Doctors Brad and Geoff Smart have made the* next quantum leap finding the keys to success in personnel selection…manpower planning; right person, right place, right tools for selection and placement. Use the knowledge in this book and you will succeed."

—John M. Eiden, President and CEO,
Continental Woodworking Co.

"If you read it with the right kind of attention, *Topgrading* is the most important book ever written."

—*Recruiter* magazine

"Of all the changes I've made to improve our company, none has been more important than topgrading. *Topgrading* (the book) is the most valuable business book I've ever read. I'd recommend it for every executive, in every company, every year!"

—Jon A. Boscia, Chairman and CEO,
Lincoln Financial Group

"No company can expect to beat the competition unless it has the best human capital and promotes these people to pivotal positions. Topgrading is the definitive manual for becoming an A player and for recognizing those traits in others."

—Larry A. Bossidy, Chairman and CEO (retired), Honeywell

if the job is a good fit for the candidate, and if the candidate is a good fit for the job. If so, *that* will become your major selling point.

Conducting an effective Topgrading interview is hard work. Even with the Topgrading Interview Guide to prompt you, it takes serious concentration. You're still trying to ask questions, listen intently, probe for details, take notes, analyze body language, pick up cues...*all at the same time.* And remember, it can take as much as four hours to conduct a quality Topgrading interview.

This explains why 95 percent of trained Topgrading interviewers strongly prefer interviewing with a tandem partner. In this case, two heads are absolutely better than one. A tandem interviewer can share the tasks of taking notes and asking questions. Your partner also can help you analyze patterns of performance that emerge.

"Apparently some human resource managers don't appreciate having interview questions answered through interpretive dance."
— Michael Hayward

"Top 3 To-Do's" for Leaders:

1. Pursue... Make the pursuit of top-flight talent your Number One Priority. Actively, aggressively seek out people for your company—or for your project team—who meet the BIW (Best in World) standard.

2. Recruit... Look at your calendar. Have you marked off large chunks of quality time for the sole, express purpose of recruiting top talent? If not, do so. Now.

3. Cut... Remove from your ranks those who don't measure up. Do it as charitably as possible, but do it with a ruthless focus on the needs of your Most Talented People (they deserve no less).

— From the "Top 10 To-Do's" for Leaders in
Tom Peters' Essentials: Leadership

Chapter 10

Use Reference Check
interviews to test
YOUR OPINIONS.

Many people have given up on reference checking, and with good reason. Traditional processes just don't make any sense. You ask a candidate to provide a list of references (like they'd voluntarily give you the names of people who'd bash them). Then, you call these references and either get a glowing endorsement or a polite statement saying they're prevented from commenting because of company policy (both equally meaningless). What a farce.

Topgrading reference checking is different. It works. And here are three reasons why it's so powerful.

- *You* decide (after the Topgrading interview) whom you want to talk with. The candidate doesn't.
- You know what to ask the references. Your questions are based on what the candidate tells you during the Topgrading interview about his or her relationships with these people.
- You ask the *candidate* to set up the Reference Check interviews. That radical idea alone can make a huge difference in your hiring effectiveness.

Use Reference Check interviews to test your opinions.

No references, no job offer. It's that simple! Hundreds of clients report that 90 percent of the references of *A* candidates will talk candidly.

Reference Check interviews are short and professional. You'll want to know:

- The situation or context they worked in with the candidate
- The candidate's strengths and weaknesses (with examples)
- How they would rate the person's overall performance in that job
- Further elaboration or insight regarding something specific the candidate admitted to struggling with in that job (a creative way of gathering more information about weaknesses)

Don't buy it when candidates say they can't provide you with references or don't know how to locate them. *A players* tend to stay in touch with their previous bosses. Even if they've lost touch, they'll be resourceful enough to find them again. Make it a condition of an employment offer, and they'll get it done.

You, or maybe your tandem interviewer, should conduct the reference calls. You did the Topgrading interview, so you're familiar with the candidate and know the data points that should be covered. As the hiring manager, you're also in the best position to make contact with previous bosses.

You'll probably have better luck if you contact the reference person at home, preferably on the weekend. Take generous notes during the call, and keep them in the candidate's file for at least six months.

Reference checks are the best way to confirm the patterns of performance you've identified in a candidate. By asking the right questions, you'll be able to round out your analysis and trust your intuition.

"I used to be a hot-tar roofer.
Yeah, I remember that day."

— Mitch Hedberg

"It's a funny thing about life; if you refuse to accept anything but the best, you very often get it."

— Somerset Maugham,
English novelist and dramatist

Chapter 11

Redeploy chronic
B AND C PLAYERS.

T O P G R A D I N G means packing teams, even the entire organization, with *A players.* As we've said, that process usually involves changing out some *Non-A's,* the chronic *B's* and *C's.* Hopefully these people can be redeployed internally into jobs where they can be *A players.* If this isn't feasible, redeploy them externally with appropriate severance and outplacement counseling.

Topgrading assessment and coaching techniques are so thorough and fair that even chronic underperformers, people who cannot be placed in jobs where they become *A's,* feel fairly treated.

Redeployment is not cruel. To the contrary, it's unkind *not* to remove *B* and *C players* and thereby imperil the jobs of everyone else. It's also unfair to leave them in the dark regarding their weaknesses and allow them to remain in jobs where they're failing.

Of course, while redeploying people externally may be the right, ethical, and legal action, the way you go about it can make a huge difference in how the action is perceived. It's a touchy situation. Let's examine it from two angles, and highlight four different approaches people use.

Redeploy chronic *B* and *C players.*

First, how easy is it for you personally to decide on the need to redeploy? Do you conscientiously assess all your people, then take your *B* and *C players* through the appropriate steps of coaching, training, and looking internally for alternative jobs? And if all those steps fail to produce an *A player,* do you readily conclude that the person has to go? Or do you waiver, procrastinate, avoid confronting issues with your *B's* and *C's,* or perhaps even ignore the fact that you have an underperformer?

The second angle relates to execution. How willing are you to take action and implement a decision to redeploy? Are you a cold sort without empathy? Or do you sympathize and show human concern, even as you deliver a clear message that the person has to go?

The following grid charts out four distinctly different redeployment styles. Read the descriptions for each one, and see which comes closest to matching your approach.

		Ease of Deciding to Redeploy	
		Easy	Hard
Ease of Implementing the Redeployment	Easy	Hatchet Person	Ostrich
	Hard	Topgrader	Wimp

"Here is Edward Bear, coming downstairs now, bump, bump, bump, on the back of his head, behind Christopher Robin. It is, as far as he knows, the only way of coming downstairs, but sometimes he feels there really is another way, if only he could stop bumping for a moment and think of it."

— A. A. Milne, *Winnie the Pooh*

The *Hatchet Person* is thorough, timely, and fair, crisply deciding to remove the *B* or *C player*. The redeployment is conducted with surgical coolness and precision. No tears, no sympathy, no delay. Team members respect the Hatchet Person's decision, but are frightened by the callous, uncaring style. Some *A players* might even find another job rather than work for such a heartless robot.

The *Wimp* frets and avoids coming to grips with *B* and *C* performance. Wimps know when they have a chronic underperfomer, but are so soft they procrastinate in making the decision to fire. They're also extremely apologetic when the deed is finally done. Team members might like Wimps as neighbors, but don't respect them as a boss or peer. The whole team suffers because Wimps give fifth and sixth chances to chronic underperformers. *A players* in the group get frustrated and look for jobs where they can be on winning teams.

Ostriches ignore evidence that they have *B* or *C players*, so they're in no position to determine if these people can be salvaged. Softness is not the problem, it's naiveté and lack of judgment. When a *C player* fails dramatically, Ostriches have no difficulty implementing a firing decision. But Ostriches are oblivious to business reality and so wrapped up in themselves that they tend to ignore the pain a *B* or *C player* will experience in being fired. Even if the Ostrich has otherwise been a Topgrader, hanging on to one *C player* might make team members consider the Ostrich a *C* as well. Inherited *A players* are apt to look for better opportunities elsewhere if the Ostrich continues to carry that *C player,* who, to the rest of the team, is an obvious underperformer.

Redeploy chronic B and C players.

The *Topgrader* is professional and caring. The *B* or *C player* has been thoroughly assessed and coached, has received a development plan, but continues to be an underperformer. The hopeless situation is recognized and dealt with properly. Topgraders do not delay the firing, but are humane. They convey a moral sense, questioning what went wrong and wondering if they could have coached better or hired better. There is genuine sympathy for the *B* or *C player's* pain. Team members respect Topgraders for their considerate manner and quick but fair decisions.

This chapter on redeployment wouldn't be necessary in a book for the entertainment industry, where it's obvious that talent counts. No one buys the CDs of *C player* musicians. The *C player* news anchor in Chicago is quickly dispatched to be a weather reporter in Peoria. Fans boo *C* athletes, while team owners and fans alike keep the heat on any manager who accepts poor performance. So why would we consider it wrong to fire employees whose work is mediocre or worse? Their continued employment is not good for the organization, not good for shareholders, not good for the team, and not good for them either.

"Sure, luck means a lot in football. Not having a good quarterback is bad luck."

— Don Shula, former head coach, Miami Dolphins

"Nothing matters more in winning than getting the right people on the field. All the clever strategies and advanced technologies in the world are nowhere near as effective without great people to put them to work."

— Jack Welch, *Winning*

Coach and keep
A PLAYERS.

It's hell trying to Topgrade if you can't hang onto your *A's* and *A potentials.* But there are several factors that conspire to create turnover in this most talented group.

To begin with, *A's* by definition are the most capable, confident, and actively recruited people. They're the ones who can most easily leave, because they have the most options.

Since your *A's* will likely be seduced at some point by others dangling job offers, you need to make sure that your opportunities remain the most appealing. Think in terms of ongoing re-recruitment. Consider what you might do to keep the *A*-types challenged, happy, and engaged. It's heartbreaking—and expensive—when one of these people walks out the door.

The irony is that your weakest and least promising employees invariably consume the biggest share of your management attention. They take the most and give the least. You worry and struggle to bring their performance up to par. Meanwhile, as you're distracted by these *B's* and *C's* you have on board, the best interests of your *A's* and *A potentials* go too long unattended. So your *A* relationships languish. These star players may begin to feel under-appreciated—taken for granted—which can make them restless and loosen the ties that bind.

Coach and keep *A players.*

You must consciously and deliberately keep the *A*-types close to you. Keep wooing them. Keep asking, "Are you happy? What do you need?" Invest yourself in helping these winners grow and succeed, rather than wasting yourself in a low payoff attempt to salvage people who more appropriately should be redeployed.

A's and *A potentials* ordinarily have a big appetite for improvement. They want to get better. So a good way to coach and keep them is to help identify and fix their most troubling weaknesses. This may run contrary to popular advice that says you should play to their strengths, but here's why it's important. *A players* already know and play to their strengths.

Therefore, most of the time you spend with *A players* on professional development should be spent helping them overcome Achilles' heels. Nothing derails management careers faster than one or two fatal flaws. Don't gnaw at *A's* about piddling things. Don't nag at them if some of their behavior just happens to annoy you personally. Focus on their most salient vulnerabilities that could sabotage their success, rather than improving things they're already good at.

It doesn't have to be all or nothing. Allocating some of your coaching time—say, ten percent—to maximizing their strengths will help maintain and build them. But your real coaching value will come from helping them with their blind spots and big weaknesses.

We divide competencies into three categories (see page 52), but these are not carved in stone! Naturally, some are easier to change through coaching than others. Also, competencies can be "relatively easy to change" or "harder but do-able" for different individuals and in different circumstances.

The "very difficult to change" list fits almost everyone. No matter how much we might want to change, there's simply no way an adult can acquire significantly more intelligence. We may learn to stretch our intelligence through hard work and listening to smart people. But it's rare for people to transform shallow analysis skills into deep ones, dullness into creativity, or lack of conceptual ability into a strength.

So to get the best return on your coaching time and effort, spend it dealing with weaknesses that are most amenable to change. Also, concentrate on key shortcomings instead of minor issues. Finally, devote the lion's share of time to your *A's* and *A potentials*. Astute, dedicated coaching helps glue them to your organization. And your job is to make the place as sticky as possible so the best talent never wants to leave.

Research shows that:

- Paper plants managed by *A players* have 94% higher profits than other paper plants.

- More talented investment banking associates are twice as productive as those average in talent.

- Return to shareholders for companies with top talent practices averages 22% above industry means.

- The top 3% of programmers produce 1200% more lines of code than the average; the top 20% produce 320% more than average.

- The top 3% of salespeople produce up to 250% more than average; the top 20% produce up to 120% more.

Coach and keep *A players.*

50 Crucial Competencies

For the "relatively easy to change" and the "harder but do-able" columns, coaching can help. The "very difficult to change" list is best addressed through appropriate hiring.

Relatively Easy to Change	Harder but Do-able	Very Difficult to Change
Risk taking	Judgment	Intelligence
Leading edge	Strategic skills	Analysis skills
Education	Pragmatism	Creativity
Experience	Track record	Conceptual ability
Organization/planning	Resourcefulness	Integrity
Self-awareness	Excellence standards	Assertiveness
Communications—oral	Independence	Inspiring followership
Communications—written	Stress management	Energy
First impression	Adaptability	Passion
Customer focus	Likability	Ambition
Political savvy	Listening	Tenacity
Selecting *A players*	Team player	
Redeploying *B/C players*	Negotiation skills	
Coaching/training	Persuasiveness	
Goal setting	Team builder	
Empowerment	Change leadership	
Performance management	Inclusivity (diversity)	
Running meetings	Conflict management	
Compatability of needs	Credible vision	
	Balance in life	

"If you think a weakness can be turned into a strength, I hate to tell you, but that's another weakness."

— Jack Handey

"Put your personnel work first because it is the most important."

— General Robert E. Wood, former president, Sears Roebuck & Company

Chapter 13

Overcome obstacles
TO TOPGRADING.

M ost managers are committed to the idea of employing highly talented people, but many find Topgrading challenging. Here are some of the most common obstacles we hear about, along with some pointed advice on how to overcome them.

1. "I can't get my *B* and *C players* to hire *A players*."

Solution A: Topgrade from the top down.

The single biggest deterrent to Topgrading is the reality that *B* and *C players* rarely hire *A's,* and *A players* rarely want to work for *B's* and *C's.* Let's say I'm a *C player.* Why would I want to hire or promote someone who could get my job? *A players* are usually perceptive enough to avoid going to work for *B's* and *C's.* *B* and *C players* are like reverse magnets to *A's*—they avoid each other.

Solution B: Require your *A players* to make the Topgrading judgments for their *B's* and *C's.*

Perhaps a *B player* will retire in two years, so *A players* can be attracted with a chance for promotion. Say to *B,* "I'll make the Topgrading judgments because you won't be around to live with the results." Then conduct a tandem Topgrading process on candidates to assess them accurately. Pairing up to do the interview lets *A players* see you're an *A* who's committed to choosing *A's* now and promoting an *A* in the near future. Steadily move the most important responsibilities from the *B player*, assigning them to the promotable *A*.

2. "We think we're hiring *A players*, but they turn out to be *B* or *C* players in disguise."

Solution: Perform more accurate assessments using the Topgrading interview, preferably in tandem.

It isn't worth the costs and hassles to remove a *B player* with only a 25 percent chance that the replacement will be an *A*. At that rate, the typical hiring manager of $100,000 people would mis-hire three and potentially waste $4.5 million to hire one *A player*. With 90 percent *A's* hired using Topgrading techniques, however, *A player* managers cull *B's* and *C's*, smoothly and quickly building a team of all *A's*.

3. "We can't afford to hire *A players.*"

Solution: Yes, you can—in fact, you already pay for *all A players.*

A's are available at all compensation levels. They are people above the 90th percentile of overall talent of all potential candidates for a given pay package. You're already paying for *A players*, whether or not you get them. So a company that's paying its *C player* marketing director a $90,000 base salary could hire an *A player* for the same salary.

But what if *A players* at $90,000 aren't good enough to beat the sophisticated competition that employs $150,000 marketing directors? In other words, let's say you can afford to hire only an *A player* in your *B* league, or a *B player* in your competition's *A* league, but realize that you need an *A player* to compete in an *A* league. Well, maybe you'd better not try to compete there head-to-head. Or perhaps you figure out how to afford the big league *A*.

Otherwise, you're probably looking at hundred-hour work weeks for yourself, plus burnout or failure for the person you underhire.

4. "I don't want to fire loyal *B* and *C players*."

Solution: Redeploy chronic *B* and *C players* because, painful as it is to fire someone, failing to do so is almost always more painful—to the company, your career, and the underperformer.

B and *C players* should be given a fair chance (though sometimes brief) to become *A players,* with extra training and coaching. If this doesn't work, it may be wise to narrow the person's job to only those responsibilities that the person can competently perform, and pay accordingly. *B* or *C players* can be considered those who are overpaid and/or underperforming. By reducing pay and/or improving performance, *B* or *C players* can become *A players.*

People are *B's* or *C's* when they're mis-hired, mis-promoted, or mis-deployed within their organizations. Not facing *your* mistakes or *your* inherited problems is *your* responsibility. Face them, or someone may conclude that you're not an *A player* either.

> "I thought I wanted to be a fireman. But as it turns out, I just like breaking windows with axes."
>
> — Buzz Nutley

"I am convinced that nothing we do is more important than hiring and developing people. At the end of the day you bet on people, not on strategies."

— Larry Bossidy, former Chairman and CEO, Honeywell

Chapter 14

Take ten steps to implement Topgrading SUCCESSFULLY.

Large and small organizations alike tend to follow a similar, logical sequence in rolling out Topgrading to make it a "way of life," not a one-time program. Common steps are:

1. All managers read *Topgrading* and work through the self-paced Topgrading DVD.

2. Senior managers participate in a Topgrading Workshop. This program explains the Topgrading vision and rollout plans, plus trains participants on how to conduct tandem Topgrading interviews and provide useful feedback/coaching.

3. Human Resources participates in a Topgrading Workshop so its staff is prepared to serve as tandem Topgrading partners and can support managers in all aspects of Topgrading.

4. All managers who have participated in a Topgrading Workshop use tandem Topgrading interviews to assess external candidates for hire. The Career History Form supplements the résumé in prescreening candidates, generating a lot more detailed information such as complete compensation history. The Topgrading Interview Guide is used for the

Topgrading interview. Reference checks are set up by the interviewee and conducted by a Topgrading interviewer using the In-Depth Reference Check Guide.

5. Topgrading professionals sometimes conduct a "second opinion" selection Topgrading interview until managers are (a) confirmed to be *A players* and (b) skilled enough that 90 percent *A players* would have been hired without the expert's assistance.

6. Topgrading professionals or internal Topgrading interviewers assess upper managers using Topgrading interviews and 360s. The CEO or top decision-maker receives an assessment report. The assessed managers receive coaching, feedback, and help preparing a comprehensive Individual Development Plan to:

- Help *A players* remain *A players* and grow.
- Help *A potentials* develop to qualify as *A players.*
- Help *B* and *C players* who will not become *A players* come to grips with the situation and recognize the need to find a job internally where they qualify as an *A player,* or leave.

7. The CEO or top decision-maker uses Topgrading to ensure a senior team of all *A players.*

8. Individual Development Plans are updated annually as part of the performance appraisal process.

9. Topgrading cascades down, throughout the organization, with steps 1-8 repeated sequentially.

10. Assessments (using tandem Topgrading interviews along with 360s) are used before every major promotion.

Finally, you need to continuously track your results. Measure your progress, at least annually, to ensure that you continue to move toward your goal of 90 percent *A's* and *A potentials*.

The idea behind Topgrading is so simple, and the payoff so remarkable, we're astounded that so few companies do it. Yet most managers at all levels still make the costly mistake of trying to "manage their way" to excellence with mediocre or poor performers on their team.

If you're serious about improving your organization's short-term and long-term performance, consider these four questions:

- Are you attracting the top 10 percent of talent available, and if not, why are you paying for *A players* and not getting them?

- Is your hiring success rate at least 90 percent, and if not, why are you not using the most advanced selection methods available to screen people?

- Do you have *B* and *C players* causing problems when, for the same salaries, *A players* could be driving performance upward?

- Would having a team of *A players* make your job easier and make managing more fun?

Take ten steps to implement Topgrading successfully.

Raise the standards for talent, and you can expect to see major performance indicators go up. We're not saying that talent is the only driver of performance. But it is a key factor, and one of the few that managers can directly control.

Truth is, you're really not in a position to affect the strength of the U.S. dollar, the whims of customers, the fierceness of competitors, or the life expectancy of products. But you can ratchet up the talent level of your organization. You can Topgrade. That will profoundly improve your leadership effectiveness and the overall success of your organization.

For more information on Topgrading tools and success stories, go to www.pritchettnet.com.

Books by PRITCHETT, LP

- *After the Merger: The Authoritative Guide for Integration Success**
- *Business As UnUsual: The Handbook for Managing and Supervising Organizational Change**
- *Carpe Mañana: 10 Critical Leadership Practices for Managing Toward the Future*
- *Culture Shift: The Employee Handbook for Changing Corporate Culture**
- *The Employee Guide to Mergers and Acquisitions**
- *The Employee Handbook for Organizational Change**
- *Shaping Corporate Culture: The Mission Critical Approach to Culture Integration and Culture Change**
- *New Work Habits for a Radically Changing World**
- *New Work Habits for The Next Millennium: 10 Ground Rules for Job Success*
- *The Ethics of Excellence*
- *Fast Growth: A Career Acceleration Strategy*
- *Firing Up Commitment During Organizational Change**
- *Hard Optimism: Developing Deep Strengths for Managing Uncertainty, Opportunity, Adversity, and Change**
- *High-Velocity Culture Change: A Handbook for Managers**
- *The Leadership Engine: Building Leaders at Every Level**
- *Making Mergers Work: A Guide to Managing Mergers and Acquisitions**
- *Managing Sideways: A Process-Driven Approach for Building the Corporate Energy Level and Becoming an "Alpha Company"**
- *The Mars Pathfinder Approach to "Faster-Better-Cheaper": Hard Proof From the NASA/JPL Pathfinder Team on How Limitations Can Guide You to Breakthroughs*
- *Mergers: Growth in the Fast Lane**
- *MindShift: The Employee Handbook for Understanding the Changing World of Work*
- *Outsourced: 12 New Rules for Running Your Career in an Interconnected World*
- *The Quantum Leap Strategy*
- *Resistance: Moving Beyond the Barriers to Change*
- *Service Excellence!**
- *Smart Moves: A Crash Course on Merger Integration Management**
- *A Survival Guide to the Stress of Organizational Change**
- *Team ReConstruction: Building a High Performance Work Group During Change**
- *Teamwork: The Team Member Handbook**
- *Topgrading: How to Hire, Coach and Keep A Players**
- *you²: A High-Velocity Formula for Multiplying Your Personal Effectiveness in Quantum Leaps*

---

*Training program also available. Please call 1-800-992-5922 for more information on our training or international rights and foreign translations.

About the Authors

Bradford D. Smart, Ph.D., is an internationally renowned management psychologist and consultant. President of Smart & Associates, Inc., he has been on the cutting-edge of executive assessment and coaching for three decades. Over the years he has conducted more than 6,500 in-depth interviews of managers for premier companies in all industries, not-for-profit organizations, and state and national governmental agencies. In a front page article,  *The Wall Street Journal* said of Brad, "He probes the executive mind—the software of business, if you will—the way a management consultant might scrutinize organizational structure and plant layout."

Brad shares his best practices for gaining a competitive talent advantage in his highly acclaimed book: *Topgrading: How Leading Companies Win by Hiring, Coaching, and Keeping the Best People.* He has brought his assessment and coaching skills to premier companies such as General Electric, Bank of America, and Honeywell. Major Topgrading programs have been credited by analysts as contributing to the successful transformation of many organizations such as Lincoln Financial Group, MarineMax, and the American Heart Assoication.

Brad holds a doctorate in industrial psychology from Purdue University. He has written two previous books on interviewing: *Selection Interviewing: A Management Psychologist's Recommended Approach,* and *The Smart Interviewer: Tools and Techniques for Hiring the Best.*

Married and the father of two grown children, Brad lives near Chicago and spends writing and free time in Northern Wisconsin and the Netherlands Antilles. Beyond the business world, he won a World Championship in Masters for springboard diving.

Geoffrey H. Smart, Ph.D., is Chairman & CEO of ghSMART, a consulting firm he founded in 1995. ghSMART is located in Chicago, Boston, Charlotte, Denver, Montreal, and New York. The firm offers quality-guaranteed services in the areas of management assessment and leadership coaching. Clients include leading venture capital and buyout investors, hedge fund managers, *Fortune* 500 senior executives, and billionaire entrepreneurs.

Formerly, Geoff worked for what is now PriceWaterhouseCoopers. He has published articles for *Fortune Small Business* and several journals of entrepreneurial finance. He co-authored the original article on Topgrading which became a best-selling management book. Geoff is a regular lecturer at Kellogg Graduate School of Management and MIT's Sloan School of Management. He serves on the Board of Directors of Junior Achievement Chicago, a not-for-profit organization whose mission is to promote an understanding of business and entrepreneurship in kids.

Geoff earned a B.A. in economics with honors from Northwestern University, an M.A. and a Ph.D. in psychology from Claremont Graduate University, where he was a student of management guru Peter F. Drucker. Geoff lives in Evergreen, CO with his wife Leslie and children.

Topgrading DVD Tool Kit

A must-have for serious Topgraders! This tool kit contains two professionally produced and edited DVDs with more than six hours of in-depth modeling, coaching, and advice from Topgrading experts Brad and Geoff Smart. It delivers a polished training seminar—without the inconvenience and expense of travel or time away from work.

The DVDs are indexed for ease of use. First, learn the Topgrading principles by working your way through each section sequentially. Later, you can go directly to the content area you need to refresh your skills.

Learn how to simplify your life and turbocharge your career by hiring, coaching, and keeping *A players!* Get smart…get skilled…and get ahead!

$1,250 per Tool Kit (plus shipping and handling)
Online licensing also available. Call for pricing and information.

SPECIAL OFFER

Order the DVD Tool Kit and receive
the following bonus Topgrading tools—all for $1,250

- The hardcover book—*Topgrading: How Leading Companies Win by Hiring, Coaching, and Keeping the Best People*—by Bradford D. Smart
- Five PRITCHETT *Topgrading* handbooks
- Three *Topgrading* CDs (seminar audio track of the DVDs)
- A one-page implementation guide
- Access to the online workbook and support tools
- An opportunity to participate in monthly coaching teleconferences throughout 2006 with Topgrading experts

To order call 1-800-992-5922 or go to www.pritchettnet.com

Topgrading

1-49 copies	____ copies at $6.95 each
50-99 copies	____ copies at $6.50 each
100-999 copies	____ copies at $5.95 each
1,000-4,999 copies	____ copies at $5.75 each
5,000-9,999 copies	____ copies at $5.50 each
10,000 or more copies	____ copies at $5.25 each

Please reference
special customer number 95TG
when ordering.

Name_____

Job Title_____

Organization_____

Address_____

City, State_____ Zip Code_____

Country_____ Phone_____ Fax_____

Email_____

Purchase order number (if applicable) _____

Applicable sales tax, shipping and handling charges will be added. Prices subject to change. Orders less than $250 require prepayment. Orders of $250 or more may be invoiced.

☐ Check Enclosed   ☐ Please Invoice

☐ **VISA**   ☐ **MasterCard**   ☐ **AMERICAN EXPRESS**

Name on Card_____

Card Number_____ Expiration Date_____

Signature_____ Date_____

TO ORDER
By phone: 800-992-5922
Online: www.pritchettnet.com
Call for our mailing address or fax number.

P R I T C H E T T
Dallas, Texas